THIS SEED OF HOPE BELONGS TO

_____

_____

_____

DEDICATION

To the Almighty God! All glory, honor, and praise belong to You. Thank You for allowing the Holy Spirit to plant this vision in my heart to create a sacred space where women can pause, reflect, and be restored through faith and written expression. This journal is a gift from You, and I offer it back to You as a vessel of healing, hope, and divine purpose.

To every woman who holds this journal, I dedicate these pages to you.
May this be more than a place to write.
May it become a sanctuary for your soul.
May your thoughts find peace,
your prayers find power,
and your journey be lit with truth.
May each page draw you closer to God's heart,
lead you in the path of righteousness,
and awaken the beauty of His promises within you.
May you find strength, grace, and clarity
as you write your way toward healing and fulfillment.
In Jesus' name. Amen.

TABLE OF CONTENTS

Dedication

Introduction

A Sacred Start

January - Healing & New Beginnings

February - Love & Identity

March - Purpose & Courage

April - Blossoming & Faith

May - Strength & Grace

June - Faith & Fruitfulness

July - Freedom & Fire

August - Wisdom & Discernment

September - Endurance in the Storm

October - Boldness & Breakthrough

November - Gratitude and Grace

December - Joy & Fulfillment

From your Heavenly Father

A Letter to Myself

Testament Page

INTRODUCTION

There are moments in life when the noise gets loud, the days get busy, and our faith feels distant. Whether you're a mother juggling responsibility, a woman facing life's storms, or someone simply in need of a sacred space to breathe and reflect. This journal was created with you in mind.

Seeds of Hope for Her is a 12-month faith-based journal designed to help you pause, reflect, and reconnect with the heart of God. Inspired by my own journey of healing and restoration, this journal invites you to plant and nurture seeds of hope through scripture, prayer, and journaling. Each month features a woman from the Bible whose story reflects strength, struggle, and triumph reminding us that we are never alone in our walk. This space is yours to write your thoughts, process your emotions, and track your spiritual growth week by week. As you journey through the year, may you begin to see your own transformation and realize how far you've come in your walk with God.

Remember:
You're powerful.
You're bold.
You're beautiful.
You're not buried; you're planted for a divine purpose.

As it says in Esther 4:14, For if you remain silent at this time, relief and deliverance for the Jews will arise from another place, but you and your father's family will perish. And who knows but that you have come to your royal position for such a time as this?"
Don't let past pain or present challenges keep you from the future God has prepared. His love is real. His Word is eternal. And this season no matter how hard will pass.

Take heart. Write honestly. Reflect deeply. And may Seeds of Hope for Her become a sacred place where you meet God, hear His voice, and grow in grace.

With love,
Etta Juah

Note: "Looking for a way to stay consistent? The Seeds of Hope Weekly Planner is a dedicated accountability tool to support your progress and deepen your daily walk. Available on Amazon just search 'Seeds of Hope Weekly Planner."

A SACRED START

"My voice shalt Thou hear in the morning, O Lord; in the morning will I direct my prayer unto Thee and will look up." — Psalm 5:3

Before the world gets your attention, give God your first breath.

This journal isn't just about writing your thoughts it's about realigning your life. Every morning is a new chance to step out of survival mode and into spiritual alignment. In the stillness before the world awakens, there is a sacred window where your soul can meet with God. It doesn't require hours. Just 15 unrushed minutes. A whisper of gratitude. One scripture. One honest prayer. One deep breath of surrender. Start your mornings not with chaos, but with Christ. Don't let your phone speak before your father does. He wants to hear your voice, not what's left over, but what's first.

Invitation:

Gratitude & Prayer: Begin by thanking God for breath, mercy, and a new start.

Word & Meditation: Feed your spirit before you feed your mind. Let Scripture reframe your thoughts.

Goal Alignment: Don't just make a list ask God, "What do You want from me today?"

Movement: Move your body, even a little. It awakens your discipline and fuels your faith.

Silence: Be still. Listen. Let God speak. In the quiet, He whispers purpose.

This is not about performance. It's about presence. You are not behind. You are not broken. You are simply being realigned.

Let this be your sacred rhythm. Let this be your new beginning. Your mornings matter because you matter.

Note: All Scriptural References are written in New International Version (NIV)

January

HEALING & NEW BEGINNINGS

"He heals the brokenhearted and binds up their wounds."
— Psalm 147:3

Woman of the Month: Naomi

Naomi's journey is one of grief transformed into grace. After losing her husband and sons, she returned to Bethlehem feeling empty and bitter, having convinced herself that her story had ended. But through Ruth's loyalty and God's Divine plan, Naomi found restoration. Though sorrow marked her journey, she never lost her quiet faith. With wisdom and humility, she guided Ruth into a future she couldn't yet see. In the end, God rewrote her story with hope, joy, and legacy. Naomi held a grandson in her arms, which also signifies the beginning of a royal legacy that would lead to Christ. Naomi reminds us that even when life feels broken, God is still at work, rewriting our stories with hope, joy, and unexpected redemption.

Looking At This Month Devotional

A New Beginning

You made it to a new year. That alone is a testament to the fact that January is often seen as a fresh start, but for many women, it also brings reminders of pain, loss, or pieces still mending. If you feel like Naomi, empty, discouraged, or worn out, know this: God is already preparing a Ruth, a Boaz, and a new chapter filled with purpose. Let Him gently restore you day by day. Permit yourself to feel, to heal, and to grow. This month, surrender to the process of becoming whole again. You are fully seen, fully loved, and never forgotten by the One who binds wounds and calls you whole. Know that: Your broken chapter isn't your final chapter.

What I Picked from Today's Devotional:

_____
_____
_____
_____
_____
_____

Prayer

"Lord, thank You for seeing me and loving me in my brokenness. Thank You for reminding me that healing is possible through You. Like Naomi, help me believe that even in seasons of loss, you are leading me into a new beginning. I step into this year with open hands and a whole heart. Continue the work You've started in me. In Jesus' name", Amen.

Further Study

Go Deeper in the Word. Take time to read Ruth chapters 1–4. Let God speak to you through Naomi's journey from bitterness to blessing.

Seed Thought: Healing is not a destination. It's a daily surrender.

QUOTE OF THE MONTH
"Even after the fall, God had a plan. Your new beginning is rooted in His redemption." - by Etta Juah

Weekly Check-ins

January
Week 1

— FAITH THAT HEALS —
SCRIPTURE OF THE WEEK:

"Daughter, your faith has healed you. Go in peace and be freed from your suffering."
– Mark 5:34

Weekly Reflections

What area of my life needs God's healing touch right now?

- ☐ Finances
- ☐ Marital
- ☐ Mental
- ☐ Emotional
- ☐ Spiritual
- ☐ Others...

Write down the specific healing focus in the category selected with Faith and Pray for God's touch over them this week.

_____
_____
_____
_____
_____
_____
_____
_____
_____

"Cast all upon Him He is the only one with a complete solution"

GRATITUDE PAGE

Dear God, thank You for this new beginning...

ADDITIONAL SEEDS NOTES

Use this space to reflect, celebrate, record answered prayers, and inspire action.

"Even after the fall, God had a plan. Your new beginning is rooted in His redemption." by Etta Juah

Weekly Check-ins

January
Week 2

── • CARRIED BY GRACE • ──
SCRIPTURE OF THE WEEK
"Come to me, all you who are weary and burdened, and I will give you rest."
– Matthew 11:28

Weekly Reflections

What burden am I carrying today that I can place in Jesus' hands?

- ☐ Am I worried?
- ☐ Am I feeling dejected?
- ☐ Am I stressed?
- ☐ Have I been let down?
- ☐ Feeling alone and lost
- ☐ Others...

Write down the burden faced within the category selected with Faith and Pray for God's touch over them this week.

_____
_____
_____
_____
_____
_____
_____
_____

"God is always there to unburden our burdens all we have to do is to speak with Him"

GRATITUDE PAGE

Dear God, thank You for this new beginning...

ADDITIONAL SEEDS NOTES

Use this space to reflect, celebrate, record answered prayers, and inspire action.

"Even after the fall, God had a plan. Your new beginning is rooted in His redemption." by Etta Juah

Weekly Check-ins

**January
Week 3**

•— RESTORED WITHIN —•
SCRIPTURE OF THE WEEK

"He restores my soul." – Psalm 23:3

Weekly Reflections

What does restoration look like for me in this season?

- ☐ Renewed
- ☐ Revived
- ☐ Reawaken
- ☐ Replaced
- ☐ Reaffirmed
- ☐ Others…

Write down the RESTORATION experience in the category selected with Faith and thank God for what He has done.

_____
_____
_____
_____
_____
_____
_____
_____
_____
_____
_____

GRATITUDE PAGE

Dear God, thank You for this new beginning...

ADDITIONAL SEEDS NOTES

Use this space to reflect, celebrate, record answered prayers, and inspire action.

"Even after the fall, God had a plan. Your new beginning is rooted in His redemption." by Etta Juah

Weekly Check-ins

January
Week 4

• A NEW THING BEGINS •
SCRIPTURE OF THE WEEK
"Forget the former things; do not dwell on the past. See, I am doing a new thing!"
– Isaiah 43:18–19

Weekly Reflections

What did God begin healing in me this month?

_____
_____
_____

What surprised me about my emotional journey?

_____
_____
_____

How do I want to grow from here?

_____
_____
_____

Breathe deeply. Sit with these questions in stillness. Then pray.

GRATITUDE PAGE

Dear God, thank You for this new beginning...

_____
_____
_____
_____
_____

ADDITIONAL SEEDS NOTES

Use this space to reflect, celebrate, record answered prayers, and inspire action.

_____
_____
_____
_____
_____
_____
_____
_____
_____

"Even after the fall, God had a plan. Your new beginning is rooted in His redemption." by Etta Juah

February

— • LOVE & IDENTITY • —

She gave this name to the Lord who spoke to her: 'You are the God who sees me,' for she said, 'I have now seen the One who sees me.'"
-Genesis 16:13

Woman of the Month: Hagar

The Woman God Saw

Alone in the desert, heart heavy and body weary, Hagar wasn't just running from Sarai; she was fleeing from rejection, shame, and confusion. A servant caught in someone else's story; she was used and cast aside. She felt invisible, unknown, and unworthy. But in the wilderness, something holy happened. God called her by name: "Hagar, where have you come from, and where are you going? Genesis 16:8". He saw her. Not just her circumstances, but her soul. Instead of rebuke, she received comfort, direction, and a promise that her son would become a great nation. Overwhelmed, Hagar did something no one in Scripture had done before: she gave God a name: El Roi, "The God who sees me." In that sacred encounter, her identity was no longer tied to rejection. It was rooted in being seen and loved by God. Hagar reminds us that our worth isn't defined by others; it's anchored in the One who knows us completely and still chooses us.

Looking At This Month Devotional

The God Who Sees You

Hagar was cast aside, rejected, and unseen by those around her. Yet in her lowest moment, God met her in the wilderness and revealed Himself as El Roi, the God who sees. Let her story remind you this month: even when you feel invisible, overlooked, or unloved, God sees every detail of your heart. He calls you by name and calls you beloved. Know that you are not forgotten. You are seen, known, and deeply loved.

Reflection

February is filled with messages about love, but true love begins with identity. The world may define love through romance, gifts, or approval, but God defines love as presence, truth, and unwavering value. Hagar wasn't anyone's first choice. She had no voice in her story, yet God gave her a divine encounter. Your identity is not found in your past, your position, or your pain. It's found in this truth: You are fully seen and deeply loved by God. This month, walk in a love that restores, not the world's version but God's. You are chosen. You are treasured. You are His.

Prayer

El Roi, the God who sees me, thank You for never leaving me unseen. In moments when I feel rejected or forgotten, remind me of who I am in You. Restore my worth, redefine my identity, and root me deeply in Your unfailing love. Like Hagar, may I rise from the wilderness with the confidence that I am seen, I am loved, and I belong to You. In Jesus' name, Amen.

Further Study

Go Deeper in the Word, take time to read more about Hagar,
Genesis 16:1–16, Genesis 21:8–21
Let God speak to you through Hagar's journey.

Seed Thought: God's love doesn't overlook you; He sees you fully and embraces you always.

QUOTE OF THE MONTH

"You are not forgotten. God's love rewrites every chapter of your life." - by Etta Juah

Weekly Check-ins

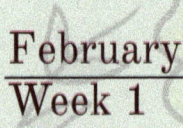

February
Week 1

———• **YOU ARE NOT BURIED, YOU ARE PLANTED IN LOVE.** •———
SCRIPTURE OF THE WEEK

"She gave this name to the Lord who spoke to her: 'You are the God who sees me,' for she said, 'I have now seen the One who sees me.'" - Genesis 16:13

Weekly Reflections

How am I beginning this month emotionally, spiritually, and mentally?

What "new thing" do I sense God doing in me?

What do I need to release in order to receive something new?

Write down your answers below:

_____
_____
_____
_____
_____
_____
_____
_____
_____
_____

GRATITUDE PAGE
Dear God, thank You for this new beginning...

ADDITIONAL SEEDS NOTES
Use this space to reflect, celebrate, record answered prayers, and inspire action.

"You are not forgotten. God's love rewrites every chapter of your life." – by Etta Juah

Weekly Check-ins

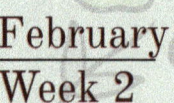

**February
Week 2**

———• GOD SEES YOU, KNOWS YOU, AND CALLS YOU WORTHY. •———
SCRIPTURE OF THE WEEK

"I have called you by name; you are mine."
-Isaiah 43:1

Prayer:
Dear God, thank You for seeing me, even in the hidden places. Help me embrace what You're planting in me this month.

Weekly Reflections

Write down the verse of the day and what stands out.
_____
_____

How does this verse speak to your current situation?
_____
_____

Ask God to help you walk in the truth of your identity.
_____
_____

Write one truth you're holding on to today.
_____
_____

List 1–3 things you're thankful for today.
_____
_____
_____

GRATITUDE PAGE
Dear God, thank You for this new beginning...

_____
_____
_____
_____

ADDITIONAL SEEDS NOTES
Use this space to reflect, celebrate, record answered prayers, and inspire action.

_____
_____
_____
_____
_____
_____
_____
_____

"You are not forgotten. God's love rewrites every chapter of your life." - by Etta Juah

Weekly Check-ins

February
Week 3

→ **YOUR PAST DOES NOT DEFINE YOUR IDENTITY, GOD'S LOVE DOES.** ←

SCRIPTURE OF THE WEEK:
God demonstrated His love while we were still sinners. -Romans 5:8

Weekly Reflections

Write down the verse of the day and what stands out.
_____

How does this verse speak to your current situation?
_____
_____

Ask God to help you walk in the truth of your identity.
_____
_____

Write one truth you're holding on to today.
_____

List 1–3 things you're thankful for today.
_____
_____
_____

GRATITUDE PAGE

Dear God, thank You for this new beginning...

_____
_____
_____
_____
_____

ADDITIONAL SEEDS NOTES

Use this space to reflect, celebrate, record answered prayers, and inspire action.

_____
_____
_____
_____
_____
_____
_____
_____

"You are not forgotten. God's love rewrites every chapter of your life." - by Etta Juah

Weekly Check-ins

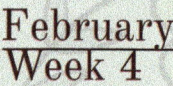

February
Week 4

→ HIDDEN PLACES ARE HOLY PLACES. YOU ARE NEVER FORGOTTEN ←
SCRIPTURE OF THE WEEK

"You have searched me, Lord, and you know me. You know when I sit and when I rise; you perceive my thoughts from afar. You discern my going out and my lying down; you are familiar with all my ways." — Psalm 139:1–3

Weekly Reflections

Write down the verse of the day and what stands out.
_____

How does this verse speak to your current situation?
_____
_____

Ask God to help you walk in the truth of your identity.
_____
_____

Write one truth you're holding on to today.
_____

List 1–3 things you're thankful for today.
_____
_____
_____

GRATITUDE PAGE

Dear God, thank You for this new beginning...

_____
_____
_____
_____
_____

ADDITIONAL SEEDS NOTES

Use this space to reflect, celebrate, record answered prayers, and inspire action.

_____
_____
_____
_____
_____
_____
_____
_____

"You are not forgotten. God's love rewrites every chapter of your life." - by Etta Juah

March

— • PURPOSE & COURAGE • —

"For if you remain silent at this time, relief and deliverance for the Jews will arise from another place, but you and your father's family will perish. And who knows but that you have come to your royal position for such a time as this?" — Esther 4:14

Woman of the Month: Esther

Stepping Boldly into Divine Assignment

Esther never dreamed she would become queen. Orphaned at a young age and raised by her cousin Mordecai, she was a Jewish girl living in a foreign land under Persian rule. Life had taught her to stay quiet, stay hidden, and stay safe. But God had other plans. When Esther was chosen to be queen, it wasn't just because of her beauty; it was because of her bravery. A time came when her people were threatened with destruction, and Esther had a choice: remain silent and protected or speak up and risk her life. Her cousin's words echoed in her heart: ("And who knows but that you have come to your royal position for such a time as this?" Esther 4:14). With trembling courage, Esther fasted, prayed, and stepped into her purpose. She approached the king without being summoned, an act punishable by death, and changed the fate of her people. Esther reminds us that courage doesn't mean the absence of fear. It means trusting God more than our fear. And walking in purpose often requires sacrifice.

Looking At This Month Devotional

Devotional: Chosen for a Purpose

Esther's story is a divine reminder that you were created with purpose and equipped with courage for the very season you're in. She didn't feel ready. She didn't feel qualified. But she decided to trust God's plan over her comfort. In a world that often pressures us to shrink back, Esther teaches us to rise. Sometimes courage looks like using your voice. Sometimes it looks like standing alone. And sometimes, courage means choosing faith even when fear is loud. God is calling you forward, not to be perfect, but to be willing. You may not have all the answers, but you have access to the One who does. If you've been questioning your place, your value, or your calling, remember this: Like Esther, your yes to God can change everything. Step forward. You're here for such a time as this.

Further Study

Go Deeper in the Word, take time to read more about Esther, Book of Esther, chapters 1–10. Emphasis (Chapter 2 -7) Let God speak to you through Esther's encounter.

Prayer

Lord, thank You for planting me in purpose, even when I don't feel ready. Give me the courage to rise like Esther, to stand boldly and trust that You have placed me here for such a time as this. Remind me daily that my obedience unlocks doors for others. Strengthen my faith, quiet my fear, and help me bloom in the place You've planted me. In Jesus' name, Amen.

Seed of Thought: You were made for this moment. Purpose lives within you, so does courage.

QUOTE OF THE MONTH

"You thought you were buried, but you were planted now rise and bloom in your purpose." by Etta Juah

Weekly Check-ins

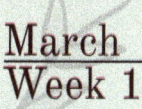

March
Week 1

→ YOU WERE CHOSEN FOR THIS MOMENT. ←
SCRIPTURE OF THE WEEK

"For if you remain silent at this time, relief and deliverance for the Jews will arise from another place, but you and your father's family will perish. And who knows but that you have come to your royal position for such a time as this?" - Esther 4:14

Weekly Reflections

How am I beginning this month emotionally, spiritually, and mentally?

- [ ] Stronger
- [ ] Better
- [ ] Tired or Weak
- [ ] Joyful
- [ ] Feeling alone and lost
- [ ] Healthy
- [ ] Others... If others fill it below

_____
_____
_____

What "new thing" do I sense God doing in me?

What do I need to release in order to receive something new?

Write down your answers below:

_____
_____
_____
_____
_____
_____
_____

GRATITUDE PAGE

Dear God, thank You for this new beginning...

_____

_____

_____

_____

ADDITIONAL SEEDS NOTES

Use this space to reflect, celebrate, record answered prayers, and inspire action.

_____

_____

_____

_____

_____

_____

_____

"You thought you were buried, but you were planted now rise and bloom in your purpose." by Etta Juah

Weekly Check-ins

**March
Week 2**

COURAGE DOESN'T MEAN THE ABSENCE OF FEAR IT MEANS OBEDIENCE DESPITE IT.

SCRIPTURE OF THE WEEK

"Have I not commanded you? Be strong and courageous. Do not be afraid; do not be discouraged, for the Lord your God will be with you wherever you go." — Joshua 1:9

Weekly Reflections

Read and reflect on today's verse.

What step of obedience is God calling you to take?   Write them below

_____
_____
_____

Write a statement of bold faith today.

_____
_____
_____

List 1–3 things you are grateful for in your journey.

_____
_____
_____

Ask God for clarity, boldness, and peace in purpose.

GRATITUDE PAGE
Dear God, thank You for this new beginning...

ADDITIONAL SEEDS NOTES
Use this space to reflect, celebrate, record answered prayers, and inspire action.

"You thought you were buried, but you were planted now rise and bloom in your purpose." by Etta Juah

Weekly Check-ins

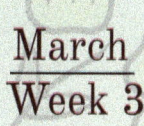

**March
Week 3**

⟶ YOUR VOICE CARRIES POWER, SPEAK BOLDLY. ⟵
SCRIPTURE OF THE WEEK:

"For the Spirit God gave us does not make us timid, but gives us power, love and self-discipline."
— 2 Timothy 1:7

Weekly Reflections

Read and reflect on today's verse.

What step of obedience is God calling you to take?   Write them below

_____
_____
_____

Write a statement of bold faith today.

_____
_____
_____

List 1–3 things you are grateful for in your journey.

_____
_____
_____

Ask God for clarity, boldness, and peace in purpose.

GRATITUDE PAGE

Dear God, thank You for this new beginning...

_____

_____

_____

_____

ADDITIONAL SEEDS NOTES

Use this space to reflect, celebrate, record answered prayers, and inspire action.

_____

_____

_____

_____

_____

_____

_____

"You thought you were buried, but you were planted now rise and bloom in your purpose." by Etta Juah

Weekly Check-ins

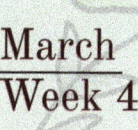

March
Week 4

—— **PURPOSE IS PLANTED IN HIS LOVE. RISE IN IT** ——
SCRIPTURE OF THE WEEK

"And we know that in all things God works for the good of those who love him, who have been called according to his purpose." — Romans 8:28

Weekly Reflections

Read and reflect on today's verse.

What step of obedience is God calling you to take?   Write them below

_____

_____

_____

Write a statement of bold faith today.

_____

_____

_____

List 1–3 things you are grateful for in your journey.

_____

_____

_____

Ask God for clarity, boldness, and peace in purpose.

GRATITUDE PAGE

Dear God, thank You for this new beginning...

_____
_____
_____
_____
_____

ADDITIONAL SEEDS NOTES

Use this space to reflect, celebrate, record answered prayers, and inspire action.

_____
_____
_____
_____
_____
_____
_____
_____

"You thought you were buried, but you were planted now rise and bloom in your purpose." by Etta Juah

April

BLOSSOMING FAITH

Jesus said to her, 'Mary.' She turned toward him and cried out in Aramaic, 'Rabboni!' (which means 'Teacher')." — John 20:16

Woman of the Month: Mary Magdalene

From Brokenness to Boldness

Mary Magdalene's life was once filled with torment. Scripture tells us she had been delivered from seven demons, a symbol of deep spiritual oppression and emotional suffering (see Luke 8:2). But everything changed when she encountered Jesus. He didn't judge her by her past. He restored her, loved her, and gave her a new identity. From that moment, Mary followed Him with deep devotion. When others fled in fear, Mary stayed. When hope seemed buried, she returned. And when the tomb was empty, it was Mary who was the first to witness the resurrected Christ. She wasn't a priest, a king, or even one of the twelve. She was a woman once overlooked by society yet chosen to carry the greatest news in history. Mary's story reminds us that you don't need a perfect past to have a powerful purpose. Faith blossoms in devotion. God uses those who are bold enough to believe Him.

Looking At This Month Devotional

The First to See Resurrection

There's something unshakable about a woman healed by Jesus. Her faith becomes bold. Her life becomes a message. Mary Magdalene teaches us that it's not about where you started, it's about who you follow. She followed Jesus when it cost her everything. She stood at the cross. She wept at the tomb. And she was called by name in resurrection glory. Blossoming faith grows through surrender, pain, and trust. Maybe this April, your heart feels dry or forgotten. But God is still at work. His Spirit is gently watering the seeds of hope within you. Let Mary's life be your reminder: your devotion matters. Even in the weeping, you will see the Lord.

Further Study

Go Deeper in the Word, take time to read:
Book of John, chapters 20 and Luke Chapter 8
Let God speak to you through Mary Magdalene's encounter.

Seed of Thought:
Who you were doesn't limit who
God is calling you to become.

Prayer

El Roi, the God who sees me, thank You for never leaving me unseen. In moments when I feel rejected or forgotten, remind me of who I am in You. Restore my worth, redefine my identity, and root me deeply in Your unfailing love. Like Hagar, may I rise from the wilderness with the confidence that I am seen, I am loved, and I belong to You. In Jesus' name, Amen.

QUOTE OF THE MONTH

"Healing begins the moment you decide to believe again." by Etta Juah

Weekly Check-ins

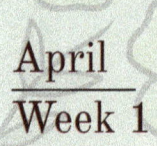

April
Week 1

— **HE CALLS YOU BY NAME: YOUR NEW BEGINNING STARTS HERE** —
SCRIPTURE OF THE WEEK

"Jesus said to her, 'Mary.' She turned toward him and cried out in Aramaic, 'Rabboni!' (which means 'Teacher')."— John 20:16

Weekly Reflections

How am I beginning this month emotionally, spiritually, and mentally?

What "new thing" do I sense God doing in me?

What do I need to release in order to receive something new?

Write down your answers below:

_____

_____

_____

_____

_____

_____

_____

_____

_____

You are not forgotten. Jesus knows you by name and meets you in your moment of need.

GRATITUDE PAGE
Dear God, thank You for this new beginning...

ADDITIONAL SEEDS NOTES
Use this space to reflect, celebrate, record answered prayers, and inspire action.

"Healing begins the moment you decide to believe again." by Etta Juah

Weekly Check-ins

April
Week 2

RESURRECTION POWER IS WORKING IN YOU
SCRIPTURE OF THE WEEK

"Therefore, if anyone is in Christ, the new creation has come: The old has gone, the new is here!"
— 2 Corinthians 5:17

Weekly Reflections

What does new life in Christ look like for me today?

How is God personally calling me this week?

What hope am I holding onto today?

Write down your answers below:

_____

_____

_____

_____

_____

_____

_____

List something new or beautiful God is doing in your life.

_____

_____

_____

The same power that raised Christ is renewing you daily. You are not who you were.

GRATITUDE PAGE
Dear God, thank You for this new beginning...

ADDITIONAL SEEDS NOTES

Use this space to reflect, celebrate, record answered prayers, and inspire action.

"Healing begins the moment you decide to believe again." by Etta Juah

Weekly Check-ins

April
Week 3

— **YOUR PAST NO LONGER DEFINES YOU. GRACE DOES.** —

SCRIPTURE OF THE WEEK

"May the God of hope fill you with all joy and peace as you trust in him, so that you may overflow with hope by the power of the Holy Spirit."— Romans 15:13

Weekly Reflections

What does living in grace look like for me today?

How is God reminding me of His power this week?

What hope is God placing in my heart right now?

Write down your answers below:

_____
_____
_____
_____
_____
_____
_____
_____

Name something beautiful blooming in this season of your life.

_____
_____

Grace rewrites your story. Hope overrules your past

GRATITUDE PAGE

Dear God, thank You for this new beginning...

ADDITIONAL SEEDS NOTES

Use this space to reflect, celebrate, record answered prayers, and inspire action.

"Healing begins the moment you decide to believe again." by Etta Juah

Weekly Check-ins

April / Week 4

● **HOPE RISES WHEN JESUS SPEAKS** ●
SCRIPTURE OF THE WEEK

"See, I am doing a new thing! Now it springs up; do you not perceive it? I am making a way in the wilderness and streams in the wasteland." — Isaiah 43:19

Weekly Reflections

What new thing is God doing in my life that I may not yet see clearly?

What wilderness am I walking through and what stream of hope has He provided?

Write down your answers below:

_____
_____
_____
_____
_____
_____
_____
_____

In what area do I need to trust His voice again?

_____
_____
_____

New beginnings don't always look like you expected but they come with God's promise.

GRATITUDE PAGE
Dear God, thank You for this new beginning...

ADDITIONAL SEEDS NOTES

Use this space to reflect, celebrate, record answered prayers, and inspire action.

"Healing begins the moment you decide to believe again." by Etta Juah

May

STRENGTH & GRACE
Faithfulness in the Field of Transition

But Ruth replied, "Don't urge me to leave you or to turn back from you. Where you go I will go, and where you stay I will stay. Your people will be my people and your God my God."-Ruth 1:16

Woman of the Month: Ruth

Strength in Surrender, Grace in Transition

Ruth's story is one of immense strength and uncommon grace. As a young widow in Moab, she faced uncertainty, loss, and an invitation to return to the familiar. Yet she chose faithfulness. She clung to Naomi, her mother-in-law, not just out of loyalty, but out of deep conviction. Ruth reminds us that every woman walks through seasons of transition, heartbreak, relocation, job changes, motherhood, grief, and growth. In those moments, like Ruth, we can choose covenant over comfort, surrender over striving, and obedience over convenience. Her choice to stay, to go with Naomi, and to serve a God she didn't fully know yet marked her forever. She became part of a redemptive lineage that brought forth King David and eventually, Jesus. Women today can relate to Ruth's journey. We all have fields where we glean, times we feel unseen, and moments where the future is foggy. Ruth teaches us that grace meets us in the field, strength rises through surrender, and legacy is born from faithfulness.

Looking At This Month Devotional

Rooted in Loyalty, Carried by Grace

Strength isn't always about what you can carry; it's about what you refuse to give up on. Grace isn't always soft; it's bold, it's holy, and it's powerful. Ruth embodied both. She could have gone back to comfort. But she chose covenant. She didn't chase a future; she trusted God to unfold it. Ruth reminds us that sometimes, the strongest women are the ones who simply keep walking in faith when they don't have all the answers. Maybe this month you feel unseen, in transition, or like you're gleaning in the fields of "just enough." But don't give up. God sees your heart, your labor, and your tears. And he is writing something beautiful with your life, something that connects to a much bigger legacy. Like Ruth, may you be rooted in love, grounded in grace, and courageous in your quiet strength. Ruth didn't need to understand the whole story to walk faithfully through her chapter. Neither do you. God honors the quiet strength of surrendered hearts.

Further Study

Read more about Ruth's story and her encounter with God in the Book of Ruth (Chapters 1–4).

Prayer

Father, thank You for being my strength when I feel weary. Thank You for surrounding me with Your grace when the road ahead is uncertain. Like Ruth, help me walk forward in faith, trusting that You have already gone before me. Teach me to be loyal, humble, and strong. I trust that my harvest is on the way. In Jesus' name, Amen.

Seed of Thought: "Strength is found in surrender, and grace blooms in the unknown. Like Ruth, we walk by faith, choosing covenant over comfort where legacy begins."

QUOTE OF THE MONTH

"Grace follows the footsteps of the faithful. Strength is built in the soil of surrender." by Etta Juah

GRATITUDE PAGE
Dear God, thank You for this new beginning...

ADDITIONAL SEEDS NOTES

Use this space to reflect, celebrate, record answered prayers, and inspire action.

"Healing begins the moment you decide to believe again." by Etta Juah

May

STRENGTH & GRACE
Faithfulness in the Field of Transition

But Ruth replied, "Don't urge me to leave you or to turn back from you. Where you go I will go, and where you stay I will stay. Your people will be my people and your God my God."-Ruth 1:16

Woman of the Month: Ruth

Strength in Surrender, Grace in Transition

Ruth's story is one of immense strength and uncommon grace. As a young widow in Moab, she faced uncertainty, loss, and an invitation to return to the familiar. Yet she chose faithfulness. She clung to Naomi, her mother-in-law, not just out of loyalty, but out of deep conviction. Ruth reminds us that every woman walks through seasons of transition, heartbreak, relocation, job changes, motherhood, grief, and growth. In those moments, like Ruth, we can choose covenant over comfort, surrender over striving, and obedience over convenience. Her choice to stay, to go with Naomi, and to serve a God she didn't fully know yet marked her forever. She became part of a redemptive lineage that brought forth King David and eventually, Jesus. Women today can relate to Ruth's journey. We all have fields where we glean, times we feel unseen, and moments where the future is foggy. Ruth teaches us that grace meets us in the field, strength rises through surrender, and legacy is born from faithfulness.

Looking At This Month Devotional

Rooted in Loyalty, Carried by Grace

Strength isn't always about what you can carry; it's about what you refuse to give up on. Grace isn't always soft; it's bold, it's holy, and it's powerful. Ruth embodied both. She could have gone back to comfort. But she chose covenant. She didn't chase a future; she trusted God to unfold it. Ruth reminds us that sometimes, the strongest women are the ones who simply keep walking in faith when they don't have all the answers. Maybe this month you feel unseen, in transition, or like you're gleaning in the fields of "just enough." But don't give up. God sees your heart, your labor, and your tears. And he is writing something beautiful with your life, something that connects to a much bigger legacy. Like Ruth, may you be rooted in love, grounded in grace, and courageous in your quiet strength. Ruth didn't need to understand the whole story to walk faithfully through her chapter. Neither do you. God honors the quiet strength of surrendered hearts.

Further Study

Read more about Ruth's story and her encounter with God in the Book of Ruth (Chapters 1–4).

Seed of Thought: "Strength is found in surrender, and grace blooms in the unknown. Like Ruth, we walk by faith, choosing covenant over comfort where legacy begins."

Prayer

Father, thank You for being my strength when I feel weary. Thank You for surrounding me with Your grace when the road ahead is uncertain. Like Ruth, help me walk forward in faith, trusting that You have already gone before me. Teach me to be loyal, humble, and strong. I trust that my harvest is on the way. In Jesus' name, Amen.

QUOTE OF THE MONTH

"Grace follows the footsteps of the faithful. Strength is built in the soil of surrender." by Etta Juah

Weekly Check-ins

May
Week 1

— YOUR STRENGTH IS IN YOUR SURRENDER —
SCRIPTURE OF THE WEEK

"But Ruth replied, 'Don't urge me to leave you or to turn back from you. Where you go, I will go, and where you stay, I will stay. Your people will be my people and your God my God." -Ruth 1:16

Weekly Reflections

How am I beginning this month emotionally, spiritually, and mentally?

What "new thing" do I sense God doing in me?

What do I need to release in order to receive something new?

Write down your answers below:

_____
_____
_____
_____
_____
_____
_____
_____
_____

What did I need God's Strength On

_____   _____

_____   _____

GRATITUDE PAGE
Dear God, thank You for this new beginning...

ADDITIONAL SEEDS NOTES

Use this space to reflect, celebrate, record answered prayers, and inspire action.

"Grace follows the footsteps of the faithful. Strength is built in the soil of surrender." by Etta Juah

Weekly Check-ins

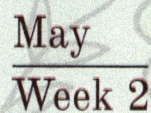

May
―――
Week 2

•―― **GRACE IS GUIDING YOUR NEXT STEP** ――•
SCRIPTURE OF THE WEEK

"Trust in the Lord with all your heart and lean not on your own understanding; in all your ways submit to him, and he will make your paths straight." -Proverbs 3:5–6

Weekly Reflections

What is God asking me to walk away from or walk toward in faith?

How have I seen grace show up in unexpected ways?

What seeds have I been planting that I need to trust God with?

Write down your answers below:

_____
_____
_____
_____
_____
_____
_____
_____
_____

Write one way you have been strong lately.

_____
_____

GRATITUDE PAGE
Dear God, thank You for this new beginning...

_____

_____

_____

_____

_____

ADDITIONAL SEEDS NOTES
Use this space to reflect, celebrate, record answered prayers, and inspire action.

_____

_____

_____

_____

_____

_____

_____

"Grace follows the footsteps of the faithful. Strength is built in the soil of surrender." by Etta Juah

Weekly Check-ins

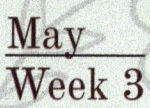

May
Week 3

• FAITHFULNESS IS NEVER WASTED •
SCRIPTURE OF THE WEEK

"Let us not become weary in doing good, for at the proper time we will reap a harvest if we do not give up."- Galatians 6:9

Weekly Reflections

What consistent effort is God calling me to remain faithful in?

What has felt hard lately that I need God's strength to continue?

What does faithfulness look like in this season?

Write down your answers below:

_____
_____
_____
_____
_____
_____
_____
_____

Places in my life where I need to rely more on God.

_____   _____

_____   _____

GRATITUDE PAGE

Dear God, thank You for this new beginning...

_____
_____
_____
_____
_____

ADDITIONAL SEEDS NOTES

Use this space to reflect, celebrate, record answered prayers, and inspire action.

_____
_____
_____
_____
_____
_____
_____
_____

"Grace follows the footsteps of the faithful. Strength is built in the soil of surrender." by Etta Juah

Weekly Check-ins

May
Week 4

• YOUR HARVEST IS COMING •
SCRIPTURE OF THE WEEK

"For the Lord God is a sun and shield; the Lord bestows favor and honor; no good thing does he withhold from those whose walk is blameless."- Psalm 84:11

Weekly Reflections

Where do I need to trust God for a harvest?

What seeds have I sown that I'm believing God to bless?

What does it mean for me to expect goodness from God?

Write down your answers below:

_____
_____
_____
_____
_____
_____
_____
_____
_____

What practical ways can I walk blamelessly and faithfully while waiting?

_____   _____

_____   _____

GRATITUDE PAGE

Dear God, thank You for this new beginning...

_____
_____
_____
_____
_____

ADDITIONAL SEEDS NOTES

Use this space to reflect, celebrate, record answered prayers, and inspire action.

_____
_____
_____
_____
_____
_____
_____

"Grace follows the footsteps of the faithful. Strength is built in the soil of surrender." by Etta Juah

June

FAITH & FRUITFULNESS
Trusting God's Timing

"Blessed is she who has believed that the Lord would fulfill his promises to her!" -Luke 1:45

Woman of the Month: Elizabeth

When Faith Outlives the Timeline

Elizabeth's life was marked by both righteousness and delay. She was faithful to God, blameless, prayerful, and deeply devoted, yet she carried the private ache of unanswered prayers. She knew the tension of trusting God while time passed her by. Still, she believed. Though barren for years, Elizabeth never let bitterness steal her belief. And in God's perfect timing, she conceived John the Baptist, becoming the mother of the prophet who would prepare the way for Christ. Her faith didn't just give birth to a child. It birthed encouragement to others. When Mary visited, pregnant with Jesus, Elizabeth was the first to recognize the presence of the Messiah. Her spiritual fruitfulness came before the physical. Elizabeth shows us that we're not forgotten in the waiting. God sees our faith even when the calendar says it's too late. Women everywhere who feel overlooked, delayed, or dried up in dreams can look to Elizabeth and know: your faith still matters. Your fruit is still coming.

Looking At This Month Devotional

When Fruitfulness Feels Delayed

Sometimes, it feels like your season of fruitfulness has passed. You've waited, prayed, and believed, yet the breakthrough hasn't arrived. Like Elizabeth, maybe you feel like time has closed the door. But God's timing isn't bound by human clocks. Elizabeth reminds us that God is not slow; He's sovereign. What looks like a delay is often divine preparation. Faith isn't passive; it's the quiet strength to keep trusting when the outcome still feels far away. Elizabeth kept walking righteously even when her womb was empty. And when God moved, He didn't just answer her prayer; He gave her a role in preparing the way for Christ. Don't give up in the in-between. Fruitfulness isn't just what grows on the outside; it's what God is cultivating in your heart, your story, and your legacy. You are not forgotten. God remembers every tear and every prayer. Your waiting is not wasted.

Further Study

Read more about Elizabeth's story and her encounter with God in the Book of Luke (Chapter 1).

Prayer

Lord, thank You for never forgetting the seeds I've sown in prayer. Like Elizabeth, I trust that Your promises never expire. Strengthen my faith during the waiting season and help me to remain expectant, joyful, and obedient. I believe that what You have spoken over my life will come to pass in Your time, not mine. In Jesus' name, Amen.

Seed of Thought: Faith doesn't expire. If God planted the promise, He would bring the fruit in His perfect time.

QUOTE OF THE MONTH

"Delay is not denial is what God promised, He will bring forth in due season." by Etta Juah

Weekly Check-ins

June
Week 1

• GOD IS NOT LATE HE'S PREPARING YOU •
SCRIPTURE OF THE WEEK

"But the angel said to him: 'Do not be afraid, Zechariah; your prayer has been heard. Your wife Elizabeth will bear you a son, and you are to call him John." - Luke 1:13

Weekly Reflections

In what area of my life do I need to trust that God's timing is better than my own?

How has God used a hidden or quiet season in my life to bring growth?

In what ways is God refining my character during this waiting season?

Write down your answers below:

_____
_____
_____
_____
_____
_____
_____
_____
_____

What promise from God am I still holding on to? How can I stay encouraged

_____   _____

_____   _____

GRATITUDE PAGE
Dear God, thank You for this new beginning...

ADDITIONAL SEEDS NOTES

Use this space to reflect, celebrate, record answered prayers, and inspire action.

"Delay is not denial is what God promised, He will bring forth in due season." by Etta Juah

Weekly Check-ins

June
Week 2

• **FRUITFULNESS BEGINS WITH FAITH** •
SCRIPTURE OF THE WEEK
"There is a time for everything, and a season for every activity under the heavens."-Ecclesiastes 3:1

Weekly Reflections

What am I still believing God for?

What promise do I need to trust again?

Where can I see God already moving?

Write down your answers below:

_____
_____
_____
_____
_____
_____
_____
_____

Thank God for the things He's growing in me.

_____   _____

_____   _____

GRATITUDE PAGE
Dear God, thank You for this new beginning...

ADDITIONAL SEEDS NOTES
Use this space to reflect, celebrate, record answered prayers, and inspire action.

"Delay is not denial is what God promised, He will bring forth in due season." by Etta Juah

Weekly Check-ins

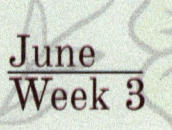

June
Week 3

── YOU ARE STILL ON HEAVEN'S CALENDAR ──
SCRIPTURE OF THE WEEK

"Let us not become weary in doing good, for at the proper time we will reap a harvest if we do not give up."-Galatians 6:9

Weekly Reflections

Where am I tempted to give up?

How can I remain faithful in the waiting?

What small seeds have I sown that I need to nurture in prayer?

Write down your answers below:

_____
_____
_____
_____
_____
_____
_____
_____

Pray for strength and courage to stay rooted in faith.

GRATITUDE PAGE

Dear God, thank You for this new beginning...

ADDITIONAL SEEDS NOTES

Use this space to reflect, celebrate, record answered prayers, and inspire action.

"Delay is not denial is what God promised, He will bring forth in due season." by Etta Juah

Weekly Check-ins

June
Week 4

— • WHAT'S GROWING IN SECRET WILL SOON BE SEEN • —
SCRIPTURE OF THE WEEK

"And by faith even Sarah, who was past childbearing age, was enabled to bear children because she considered him faithful who had made the promise." -Hebrews 11:11

Weekly Reflections

What have I been nurturing quietly that God is calling into bloom?

How can I trust His timing over my timeline?

What lesson am I learning in this season of quiet growth?

Write down your answers below:

_____
_____
_____
_____
_____
_____
_____
_____
_____
_____

Thank God for hidden growth and ask Him for eyes to see His faithfulness.

GRATITUDE PAGE

Dear God, thank You for this new beginning...

ADDITIONAL SEEDS NOTES

Use this space to reflect, celebrate, record answered prayers, and inspire action.

"Delay is not denial is what God promised, He will bring forth in due season." by Etta Juah

Weekly Check-ins

June / Week 4

• WHAT'S GROWING IN SECRET WILL SOON BE SEEN •
SCRIPTURE OF THE WEEK

"And by faith even Sarah, who was past childbearing age, was enabled to bear children because she considered him faithful who had made the promise." -Hebrews 11:11

Weekly Reflections

What have I been nurturing quietly that God is calling into bloom?

How can I trust His timing over my timeline?

What lesson am I learning in this season of quiet growth?

Write down your answers below:

_____
_____
_____
_____
_____
_____
_____
_____
_____
_____
_____

Thank God for hidden growth and ask Him for eyes to see His faithfulness.

GRATITUDE PAGE

Dear God, thank You for this new beginning...

ADDITIONAL SEEDS NOTES

Use this space to reflect, celebrate, record answered prayers, and inspire action.

"Delay is not denial is what God promised, He will bring forth in due season." by Etta Juah

July

FREEDOM & FIRE
Rising with Courage and Authority

"Villagers in Israel would not fight; they held back until I, Deborah, arose, until I arose, a mother in Israel." — Judges 5:7 (NIV)

Woman of the Month: Deborah

A Woman of Freedom and Fire
In a time of national paralysis and spiritual drought, Deborah emerged like a spark in the dark. She wasn't just a judge; she was a prophetess, a leader, a mother in Israel. When everyone else was silent, she spoke. When fear gripped men like Barak, she stood in confidence, declaring the word of the Lord. Deborah didn't ask for permission to rise; she simply rose. And in doing so, she ignited a movement. Her story is proof that freedom and fire flow through the woman who walks in divine authority. Like Deborah, many women today feel the call to rise to speak, lead, create, or rebuild, but are met with hesitation, resistance, or fear. But when you understand your God-given identity and authority, your voice becomes a weapon, your obedience a spark, and your life a fire that sets others free.

Looking At This Month Devotional

Leading with Fire, Walking in Freedom
"When the princes in Israel take the lead, when the people willingly offer themselves praise the Lord Judges 5:2". Freedom isn't just about breaking free from something; it's about rising into something greater. God is raising modern-day Deborahs women who carry fire in their bones and courage in their voices. Maybe your past has tried to silence you. Maybe you've been told you're too strong, too loud, too different. But like Deborah, your power isn't rooted in people's permission; it's rooted in God's call. This month, let every hesitation burn away. Let every fear be consumed. Step boldly into the fire of your calling. You were born to lead. You were born to burn.

Take note: Walk in spiritual authority like Deborah. Let your obedience set others free. God will use your boldness to bring victory. Freedom begins with saying "yes" to the fire inside you.

Further Study

Read More About Deborah's Story and Encounter with God In Judges chapters 4 and 5.

Seed of Thought "You're a torchbearer don't dim your fire. God called you not just to be free, but to lead others to freedom.

Prayer

God of justice and fire, thank You for the boldness of Deborah. Let her story ignite a fire in me to rise in courage, speak with clarity, and lead without fear. Teach me to trust that You've already gone before me. I receive Your freedom and walk forward in spiritual authority. Let every step I take set others free. In Jesus' name, Amen.

QUOTE OF THE MONTH
"When you rise in your calling, you set others free to rise in theirs." by Etta Juah

Weekly Check-ins

July
Week 1

• YOU WERE BORN TO LEAD WITH BOLDNESS •
SCRIPTURE OF THE WEEK

"Now Deborah, a prophet, the wife of Lappidoth, was leading Israel at that time." — Judges 4:4

Weekly Reflections

How am I beginning this month emotionally, spiritually, and mentally?

What "new thing" do I sense God doing in me?

What do I need to release in order to receive something new?

Write down your answers below:

_____
_____
_____
_____
_____
_____
_____
_____
_____
_____

Use this space to reflect:

GRATITUDE PAGE
Dear God, thank You for this new beginning...

_____
_____
_____
_____
_____

ADDITIONAL SEEDS NOTES
Use this space to reflect, celebrate, record answered prayers, and inspire action.

_____
_____
_____
_____
_____
_____
_____
_____

"When you rise in your calling, you set others free to rise in theirs." by Etta Juah

Weekly Check-ins

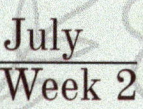

July
Week 2

→ THERE IS FIRE IN YOUR VOICE AND FREEDOM IN YOUR OBEDIENCE ←
SCRIPTURE OF THE WEEK

"The Spirit of the Sovereign Lord is on me, because the Lord has anointed me to proclaim good news to the poor. He has sent me to bind up the brokenhearted, to proclaim freedom for the captives and release from darkness for the prisoners…" — Isaiah 61:1

Weekly Reflections

What is God asking me to obey, even if it's uncomfortable?

How can I be more intentional with what I say and how I say it?

Am I boldly using my voice to speak life, truth, and purpose?

Write down your answers below:

_____
_____
_____
_____
_____
_____
_____
_____
_____

Declare one truth about the power you carry in Christ.
_____

Ask for boldness, clarity, and fire to lead well.

GRATITUDE PAGE

Dear God, thank You for this new beginning...

_____
_____
_____
_____

ADDITIONAL SEEDS NOTES

Use this space to reflect, celebrate, record answered prayers, and inspire action.

_____
_____
_____
_____
_____
_____
_____

"When you rise in your calling, you set others free to rise in theirs." by Etta Juah

Weekly Check-ins

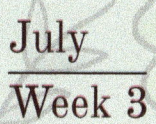

July

Week 3

• YOU CARRY HEAVEN'S AUTHORITY WALK IN IT •
SCRIPTURE OF THE WEEK
"But you will receive power when the Holy Spirit comes on you; and you will be my witnesses…" — Acts 1:8

Weekly Reflections

Where is God calling me to be bold this week?

What mindset or fear do I need to let go of?

What is one thing I'm celebrating in my leadership or personal growth journey today?

Write down your answers below:

_____
_____
_____
_____
_____
_____
_____
_____
_____

Declare one truth about the power you carry in Christ.
_____

Ask for boldness, clarity, and fire to lead well.

GRATITUDE PAGE

Dear God, thank You for this new beginning...

ADDITIONAL SEEDS NOTES

Use this space to reflect, celebrate, record answered prayers, and inspire action.

"When you rise in your calling, you set others free to rise in theirs." by Etta Juah

Weekly Check-ins

July
Week 4

BOLD FAITH UNLOCKS BREAKTHROUGH
SCRIPTURE OF THE WEEK

"No, in all these things we are more than conquerors through him who loved us." — Romans 8:37 (NIV)

Weekly Reflections

What promise do I need to boldly believe again?

What step is fear holding me back from taking?

How can I choose bold, steady faith in this season?

Write down your answers below:

_____
_____
_____
_____
_____
_____
_____
_____

What comfort zone is God asking me to step out of?

_____   _____

_____   _____

GRATITUDE PAGE

Dear God, thank You for this new beginning...

ADDITIONAL SEEDS NOTES

Use this space to reflect, celebrate, record answered prayers, and inspire action.

"When you rise in your calling, you set others free to rise in theirs." by Etta Juah

August

WISDOM & DISCERNMENT
Calm in the Storm, Wisdom in the Moment

"May you be blessed for your good judgment and for keeping me from bloodshed this day and from avenging myself with my own hands." — 1 Samuel 25:33

Woman of the Month: Abigail

A Portrait of Discernment
In a time when impulsive decisions could mean the loss of many lives, Abigail stood out as a woman of poise and deep discernment. Married to Nabal, a man known for his foolishness, Abigail didn't allow her environment to dictate her character. When David, future king of Israel, was on his way to destroy her household in anger, Abigail intercepted him with wisdom, humility, and a peace offering. He reminded David of who he was in God's plan and helped him avoid bloodshed, becoming a divine interruption to a disastrous decision. Her wisdom protected lives and aligned her with God's greater purpose. Like Abigail, every woman today holds the potential to speak peace, walk in divine timing, and protect destinies through discernment and grace.

Looking At This Month Devotional

The Power of a Discerning Spirit
"May you be blessed for your good judgment and for keeping me from bloodshed this day and from avenging myself with my own hands 1 Samuel 25:33". In today's chaotic world, wisdom is not just knowledge; it is Spirit-led action. Abigail teaches us that discernment is about knowing when and how to move. She wasn't frantic or fearful. Instead, she responded to the crisis with calm and clarity. Her words turned David's anger into blessing and saved her entire household. God is still raising women like Abigail, those who stand strong in grace, speak peace in storms, and operate with divine insight. This month, may you be sensitive to the Spirit, ready to speak wisely, and bold to act when God calls. Your wisdom could be the answer to a battle you didn't even know was coming. Discernment isn't passive; it's powerful. With God, your peace can protect more than just you.

Further Study

Read more about Abigail's story and her encounter with God in 1 Samuel 25.

Prayer

Father of Wisdom, thank You for the spirit of discernment that you give freely to those who ask. Make me more like Abigail steadfast, wise, and full of grace. Teach me to listen before I speak and to move with courage when it's time to act. Let my words be full of peace and my actions grounded in truth. In Jesus' name, Amen.

Seed of Thought: Sometimes, wisdom means taking the first step calmly, quietly, and courageously.

QUOTE OF THE MONTH

"A wise woman doesn't just speak peace she carries it into every room she enters." Etta Juah

Weekly Check-ins

August
Week 1

WISDOM IS YOUR WEAPON DISCERNMENT IS YOUR SHIELD
SCRIPTURE OF THE WEEK

"His name was Nabal and his wife's name was Abigail. She was an intelligent and beautiful woman, but her husband was surly and mean in his dealings."— 1 Samuel 25:3

Weekly Reflections

How am I beginning this month emotionally, spiritually, and mentally?

What "new thing" do I sense God doing in me?

How can I ask God for sharper spiritual discernment today

Write down your answers below:

_____
_____
_____
_____
_____
_____
_____
_____
_____

Where is God asking me to pause and listen before acting?

_____
_____

GRATITUDE PAGE

What Are You Grateful For This Week

_____
_____
_____
_____
_____

ADDITIONAL SEEDS NOTES

Use this space to reflect, celebrate, record answered prayers, and inspire action.

_____
_____
_____
_____
_____
_____
_____
_____

"A wise woman doesn't just speak peace she carries it into every room she enters." Etta Juah

Weekly Check-ins

August
Week 2

SPEAK PEACE EVEN IN HEATED PLACES
SCRIPTURE OF THE WEEK

"The wise woman builds her house, but with her own hands the foolish one tears hers down."— Proverbs 14:1

Weekly Reflections

Where can I choose wisdom over reaction today?

How can I bring calmness into a situation or relationship this week?

What is one area in my life where I need clarity or spiritual insight right now?

Write down your answers below:

_____
_____
_____
_____
_____
_____
_____
_____
_____

Celebrate a recent wise decision or peaceful outcome.

Have I asked God to increase my wisdom and guide my actions today?

GRATITUDE PAGE
What are you thankful for this week

ADDITIONAL SEEDS NOTES
Use this space to reflect, celebrate, record answered prayers, and inspire action.

"A wise woman doesn't just speak peace she carries it into every room she enters." Etta Juah

Weekly Check-ins

August
Week 3

THE WISE WOMAN BUILDS HER HOUSE WITH QUIET STRENGTH
SCRIPTURE OF THE WEEK

"If any of you lacks wisdom, you should ask God, who gives generously to all without finding fault, and it will be given to you."— James 1:5

Weekly Reflections

How can I embrace quiet strength in my words, choices, or leadership?

In what area of my life am I being called to build rather than tear down?

Are there any words I need to take back, or start speaking to build wisely?

Write down your answers below:

_____
_____
_____
_____
_____
_____
_____
_____
_____

How can you stay spiritually rooted while building your house and purpose?

_____
_____

GRATITUDE PAGE
What are you thankful for this week

_____
_____
_____
_____
_____

ADDITIONAL SEEDS NOTES

Use this space to reflect, celebrate, record answered prayers, and inspire action.

_____
_____
_____
_____
_____
_____
_____
_____

"A wise woman doesn't just speak peace she carries it into every room she enters." Etta Juah

Weekly Check-ins

August / Week 4

— DISCERNMENT WILL TAKE YOU WHERE EMOTIONS CAN'T —
SCRIPTURE OF THE WEEK

"Trust in the Lord with all your heart and lean not on your own understanding; in all your ways submit to him, and he will make your paths straight."—Proverbs 3:5–6 (NIV)

Weekly Reflections

Where have I allowed emotions to lead, and how can I invite God's clarity instead?

In what situation do I need to slow down and seek God's discernment before responding?

What decision am I facing right now that needs spiritual insight, not emotional reaction?

Write down your answers below:

_____

_____

_____

_____

_____

_____

_____

_____

_____

How can you stay spiritually rooted while building your house and purpose?

_____

_____

GRATITUDE PAGE
What are you thankful for this week

ADDITIONAL SEEDS NOTES
Use this space to reflect, celebrate, record answered prayers, and inspire action.

"A wise woman doesn't just speak peace she carries it into every room she enters." Etta Juah

September

ENDURANCE IN THE STORM
Reaching for Wholeness

"Then he said to her, 'Daughter, your faith has healed you. Go in peace.'" — Luke 8:48

Woman of the Month: The Woman with the Issue of Blood

An Enduring Faith in Action

She had no name to the people around her. For twelve long years, she was known by her condition of bleeding. Labeled unclean, she was cut off from family, community, and temple worship. Every doctor she had seen failed her. She spent everything she had, yet only grew worse. Still, she hoped. When she heard Jesus was near, she didn't wait for an invitation. She pressed through the crowd, shame and fear clinging to her like a cloak, and with trembling faith, she reached for the hem of His robe. Immediately, she was healed. But Jesus wanted more than a miracle. He wanted her heart. He stopped, looked for her, and called her Daughter. That one word restored not just her health but her identity. Her story is every woman's story who has silently suffered, who has held onto hope in the dark, who dared to believe again. This month, may her story inspire us to reach even when it hurts.

Looking At This Month Devotional

The Faith to Reach Again

"He said to her, 'Daughter, your faith has healed you. Go in peace and be freed from your suffering Mark 5:34". Her storm lasted twelve long years. The kind of storm that isolates you, weakens you, and drains every ounce of your hope. But the moment she reached for Jesus, everything changed. Endurance doesn't always look like strength. Sometimes, it looks like crawling through a crowd. Sometimes, it's whispering a prayer when you feel like God is silent. But that moment of reaching is powerful. Because Jesus still responds to desperate, faith-filled touches. If you're in a storm right now, this month is for you. Don't stop reaching. Your faith still touches heaven.

Endurance is not passive; it's active, even in weakness, Jesus doesn't just heal bodies; He restores identities. You don't need the loudest voice, just enough faith to reach

Further Study

Read more about her encounter with Jesus: Mark 5:25–34, and Luke 8:43–48

Seed of Thought: What if your healing begins not with a breakthrough, but with a reach?

Prayer

Jesus, I come to You like the woman who reached out in faith, believing there is more beyond the pain. Heal every hidden place, restore what has been broken, and call me "daughter" again. I trust you to restore not just my body, but my soul. Thank You for peace, for presence, and for wholeness. In Your name, Amen.

QUOTE OF THE MONTH

"Don't quit in the middle of your healing. Hope is still reaching for you." by Etta Juah

Weekly Check-ins

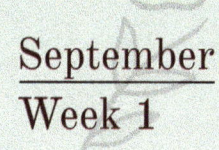

September
Week 1

— HEALING BEGINS WITH A REACH —
SCRIPTURE OF THE WEEK

"And a woman was there who had been subject to bleeding for twelve years, but no one could heal her. She came up behind him and touched the edge of his cloak, and immediately her bleeding stopped. 'Who touched me?' Jesus asked… Then he said to her, 'Daughter, your faith has healed you. Go in peace.'" — Luke 8:43–48

Weekly Reflections

Where in my heart do I need to reach out and touch God's grace?

What pain or burden am I ready to lay at His feet today?

Am I trying to heal on my own, or have I truly reached out in surrender?

Write down your answers below:

_____
_____
_____
_____
_____
_____
_____
_____

What progress in my healing journey can I thank God for today?

_____

GRATITUDE PAGE

What are you thankful for this week

ADDITIONAL SEEDS NOTES

Use this space to reflect, celebrate, record answered prayers, and inspire action.

"Don't quit in the middle of your healing. Hope is still reaching for you." by Etta Juah

Weekly Check-ins

September
Week 2

YOU ARE NOT FORGOTTEN: YOU ARE BEING RESTORED
SCRIPTURE OF THE WEEK

"But I will restore you to health and heal your wounds,' declares the Lord." — Jeremiah 30:17

Weekly Reflections

When was the last time I felt forgotten, and how can I trust that God sees me now?

What promise or truth can I hold onto as I wait for full restoration?

What lie about my worth do I need to replace with God's truth?

Write down your answers below:

_____
_____
_____
_____
_____
_____
_____
_____
_____

How is this season shaping me for what I've been praying for?

_____
_____

GRATITUDE PAGE

What are you thankful for this week

_____
_____
_____
_____

ADDITIONAL SEEDS NOTES

Use this space to reflect, celebrate, record answered prayers, and inspire action.

_____
_____
_____
_____
_____
_____
_____

"Don't quit in the middle of your healing. Hope is still reaching for you." by Etta Juah

Weekly Check-ins

September
Week 3

— THERE IS PEACE BEYOND THE PAIN —
SCRIPTURE OF THE WEEK

"He heals the brokenhearted and binds up their wounds." — Psalm 147:3

Weekly Reflections

What broken places am I still carrying?

How is God inviting me to peace right now?

What am I learning about God's character in my storm?

Write down your answers below:

_____

_____

_____

_____

_____

_____

_____

Write 1–3 things you're grateful for even in your healing process.

_____

_____

_____

GRATITUDE PAGE
What are you thankful for this week

ADDITIONAL SEEDS NOTES

Use this space to reflect, celebrate, record answered prayers, and inspire action.

"Don't quit in the middle of your healing. Hope is still reaching for you." by Etta Juah

Weekly Check-ins

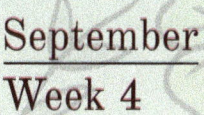

September
Week 4

• YOUR FAITH STILL TOUCHES HEAVEN •
SCRIPTURE OF THE WEEK

"But he was pierced for our transgressions, he was crushed for our iniquities; the punishment that brought us peace was on him, and by his wounds we are healed." — Isaiah 53:5

Weekly Reflections

In what areas do I need to reach out to Jesus again?

What does "being called Daughter" mean to me personally?

How can I continue to trust God even when I don't feel strong?

Write down your answers below:

_____
_____
_____
_____
_____
_____
_____
_____

What have I stopped praying for that I need to lift up again in faith?

_____

How is my faith planting seeds for those who come after me?

_____

GRATITUDE PAGE

What are you thankful for this week

_____
_____
_____
_____
_____

ADDITIONAL SEEDS NOTES

Use this space to reflect, celebrate, record answered prayers, and inspire action.

_____
_____
_____
_____
_____
_____
_____

"Don't quit in the middle of your healing. Hope is still reaching for you." by Etta Juah

October

BOLDNESS & BREAKTHROUGH
Victory in Unlikely Hands

"Most blessed of women be Jael, the wife of Heber the Kenite, most blessed of tent-dwelling women." — Judges 5:24

Woman of the Month: Jael

A Woman of Quiet Courage and Daring Obedience

When we think of boldness, we often imagine loud, visible strength. But the story of Jael, tucked in the book of Judges, shows us a different kind. Jael was not a warrior, prophetess, or public leader. She was a tent-dwelling woman, quietly positioned, unnoticed by many, yet powerfully used by God. Her home became a battleground, and her hands became God's weapon of breakthrough. She discerned the moment. She didn't wait for someone else to act. She aligned with God's purpose and delivered victory for a nation. Women today can deeply relate to Jael those who are often overlooked, yet faithfully watching and ready. Women who may not carry titles but carry divine assignments. Her story reminds us: You don't have to be loud to be brave. You just have to be available when God calls.

Looking At This Month Devotional

Courage in Unexpected Places

"Most blessed of women be Jael, the wife of Heber the Kenite, most blessed of tent-dwelling women. He asked for water, and she gave him milk; in a bowl fit for nobles, she brought him curdled milk. Her hand reached for the tent peg, her right hand for the workman's hammer. She struck Sisera, she crushed his head, she shattered and pierced his temple." (Judges 5:24-26). Sometimes, God positions you in places that seem too ordinary to matter, but He has extraordinary plans for you there. Jael didn't ask for the moment; it came to her. And when it did, she didn't panic she acted. With courage in her heart and discernment in her spirit, she struck a blow that would end oppression and usher in peace. Your breakthrough might not look like a battlefield, but maybe it's a conversation, a choice, a prayer, a stand you need to take. Boldness isn't always loud it's faithful. It's the woman who rises when everyone else shrinks back. The one who obeys God when fear is loud and strength feels small.

Further Study

Read More: Jael's Story & Encounter with God
Discover Jael's full story in Judges 4–5.

Seed of Thought: Boldness is not about being fearless; it's about saying yes to God in the face of fear.

Prayer

Lord, give me the spirit of Jael quiet strength, divine courage, and fearless obedience. Help me to recognize the moments You place in my hands and to respond with boldness and faith. I trust you to bring breakthrough through my yes. Make me bold, make me ready, and make me victorious in You. In Jesus' name, Amen.

QUOTE OF THE MONTH

"When God places the moment in your hands, don't shrink—strike with boldness." - Etta Juah

Weekly Check-ins

October
Week 1

———• BOLDNESS IS OBEDIENCE IN MOTION •———
SCRIPTURE OF THE WEEK

"But Jael, Heber's wife, picked up a tent peg and a hammer and went quietly to him while he lay fast asleep, exhausted. She drove the peg through his temple into the ground, and he died." — Judges 4:21

Weekly Reflections

How am I beginning this month emotionally, spiritually, and mentally?

Where is God asking me to take a bold step of obedience right now?

What action have I been delaying that obedience is calling me to take?

Write down your answers below:

_____
_____
_____
_____
_____
_____
_____

How have I been playing it safe, and what would bold obedience look like instead?

_____

How can I put action to my "yes" this week even in small ways?

_____

GRATITUDE PAGE
What are you thankful for this week

ADDITIONAL SEEDS NOTES

Use this space to reflect, celebrate, record answered prayers, and inspire action.

"When God places the moment in your hands, don't shrink—strike with boldness." - Etta Juah

Weekly Check-ins

October
Week 2

GOD GIVES ORDINARY HANDS EXTRAORDINARY POWER
SCRIPTURE OF THE WEEK

"Have I not commanded you? Be strong and courageous. Do not be afraid; do not be discouraged, for the Lord your God will be with you wherever you go." — Joshua 1:9 NIV

Weekly Reflections

Where do I need to rise in boldness today?

What do I believe God is preparing me to overcome?

Declare a breakthrough I'm praying for and trusting God to deliver.

Write down your answers below:
_____
_____
_____
_____
_____
_____
_____

Write down one bold step I will take this week.
_____
_____

Ask for the boldness to step forward and the discernment to act.

GRATITUDE PAGE

What are you thankful for this week

_____
_____
_____
_____
_____

ADDITIONAL SEEDS NOTES

Use this space to reflect, celebrate, record answered prayers, and inspire action.

_____
_____
_____
_____
_____
_____
_____
_____

"When God places the moment in your hands, don't shrink—strike with boldness." - Etta Juah

Weekly Check-ins

**October
Week 3**

• YOUR YES CAN BREAK STRONGHOLDS •
SCRIPTURE OF THE WEEK

"So do not fear, for I am with you; do not be dismayed, for I am your God. I will strengthen you and help you; I will uphold you with my righteous right hand." — Isaiah 41:10

Weekly Reflections

What area of my life needs a surrendered "yes" today?

What stronghold in my life is being broken by my consistent obedience?

Who might be impacted by the yes I've been hesitating to give?

Write down your answers below:

_____
_____
_____
_____
_____
_____
_____
_____

What excuse or fear have I been using to delay my yes?

_____

How can I keep my heart in a posture of daily, willing surrender?

_____

GRATITUDE PAGE

What are you thankful for this week

_____

_____

_____

_____

ADDITIONAL SEEDS NOTES

Use this space to reflect, celebrate, record answered prayers, and inspire action.

_____

_____

_____

_____

_____

_____

_____

"When God places the moment in your hands, don't shrink—strike with boldness." - Etta Juah

Weekly Check-ins

October
Week 4

• FEAR FLEES WHERE BOLD FAITH STANDS •
SCRIPTURE OF THE WEEK

"He trains my hands for battle; my arms can bend a bow of bronze." — Psalm 18:34

Weekly Reflections

What truth do I need to stand on today to silence fear?

Am I allowing fear to speak louder than the Spirit within me?

What fearful lie do I need to replace with God's truth?

Write down your answers below:

_____
_____
_____
_____
_____
_____
_____

How is this difficult season strengthening my faith?

_____

How can I let my faith shine more boldly today?

_____

GRATITUDE PAGE

What are you thankful for this week

_____
_____
_____
_____

ADDITIONAL SEEDS NOTES

Use this space to reflect, celebrate, record answered prayers, and inspire action.

_____
_____
_____
_____
_____
_____
_____
_____

"When God places the moment in your hands, don't shrink—strike with boldness." - Etta Juah

November

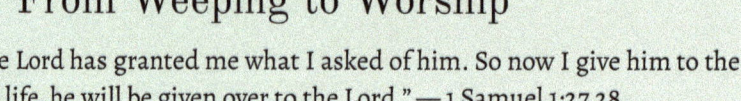
GRATITUDE & GRACE
From Weeping to Worship

"I prayed for this child, and the Lord has granted me what I asked of him. So now I give him to the Lord. For his whole life, he will be given over to the Lord." — 1 Samuel 1:27 28

Woman of the Month: Hannah

Worship That Was Born in Tears

Before there was praise, there was pain. Before Samuel, there were silent years filled with weeping, longing, and misunderstanding. Hannah's story is one of raw emotion and holy surrender. She was mocked by others, misunderstood by spiritual leaders, and still, she faithfully returned to the presence of God. Her quiet persistence in prayer became the very place where heaven touched earth. Women today can relate to Hannah's mix of sorrow and hope. We've all had seasons where we carried unspoken burdens, where joy seemed delayed. And yet, like Hannah, our grace story often begins in our weeping when we dare to pour out our soul before the Lord. What sets Hannah apart is not only her answered prayer but what she did afterward. She kept her vow. She gave the blessing back. And from her womb came a prophet who changed Israel's history. Hannah shows us that gratitude doesn't wait until the story is perfect. It rises from surrender and transforms even tears into worship.

Looking At This Month Devotional

Worship Through the Waiting

"I prayed for this child, and the Lord has granted me what I asked of him." (1 Samuel 1:27). Hannah didn't sugarcoat her pain. She wept. She prayed. And she trusted. Waiting is never easy. But grace meets us in those waiting rooms of life, not with instant answers, but with the strength to keep believing. Gratitude doesn't deny the struggle; it acknowledges God's faithfulness within it. When God answered Hannah's prayer, she did the unthinkable she gave the child back. That's worship. She understood that every good gift is from above, and nothing we surrender to God is ever lost. So, whether you are in a season of weeping or rejoicing, take a moment to worship. Offer what you have your hopes, your grief, your gratitude and let grace cover the rest. God welcomes your raw, honest prayers. Gratitude is not a feeling it's a posture of faith What you release to God, He multiplies. Grace often shows up in quiet, persistent surrender.

Further Study

Read more about Hannah's encounter with God: 1 Samuel Chapter 1–2

Seed of Thought: Worship begins when we trust God with both our tears and our treasures.

Prayer

Faithful Father, thank You for hearing my prayers, even when they are soaked in tears. Like Hannah, help me to worship in the waiting and surrender in the receiving. Teach me to hold blessings with open hands and to trust You in all things. Fill my heart with thanksgiving and my life with grace. In Jesus' name, Amen.

QUOTE OF THE MONTH

"Gratitude is the song of the soul that remembers who held it through the storm." - Etta Juah

Weekly Check-ins

November
Week 1

• GOD HEARS THE QUIETEST CRIES OF YOUR HEART •
SCRIPTURE OF THE WEEK

"In her deep anguish, Hannah prayed to the Lord, weeping bitterly." — 1 Samuel 1:10

Weekly Reflections

How am I beginning this month emotionally, spiritually, and mentally?

When was the last time I let God hear my unspoken cry?

What hidden burden do I need to lay at God's feet?

Write down your answers below:

_____
_____
_____
_____
_____
_____
_____
_____

Am I being real with God, or just saying what sounds right?

_____

What is my soul whispering to God today?

_____

GRATITUDE PAGE
What are you thankful for this week

_____

_____

_____

_____

ADDITIONAL SEEDS NOTES
Use this space to reflect, celebrate, record answered prayers, and inspire action.

_____

_____

_____

_____

_____

_____

_____

"Gratitude is the song of the soul that remembers who held it through the storm." - Etta Juah

Weekly Check-ins

November
Week 2

• **YOUR TEARS WATER THE SOIL OF ANSWERED PRAYER** •
SCRIPTURE OF THE WEEK

"Do not be anxious about anything, but in every situation, by prayer and petition, with thanksgiving, present your requests to God." — Philippians 4:6

Weekly Reflections

What am I most thankful for today big or small?

What am I still trusting God to answer?

Where have I seen God's grace carry me this year?

Write down your answers below:

_____
_____
_____
_____
_____
_____
_____
_____

What do I need to give back to God in trust?
_____

Write a short praise or worship declaration:
_____

GRATITUDE PAGE
What are you thankful for this week

ADDITIONAL SEEDS NOTES

Use this space to reflect, celebrate, record answered prayers, and inspire action.

"Gratitude is the song of the soul that remembers who held it through the storm." - Etta Juah

Weekly Check-ins

November
Week 3

• GRATITUDE IS THE GATEWAY TO DEEPER GRACE •
SCRIPTURE OF THE WEEK

"Enter his gates with thanksgiving and his courts with praise; give thanks to him and praise his name." — Psalm 100:4

Weekly Reflections

What am I most thankful for today big or small?

How has God's grace surprised me recently?

In what area of my life have I seen increase through gratitude?

Write down your answers below:

_____

_____

_____

_____

_____

_____

_____

What dark moment did gratitude help me overcome?

_____

What joy has flowed from choosing to be grateful?

_____

GRATITUDE PAGE

What are you thankful for this week

_____
_____
_____
_____
_____

ADDITIONAL SEEDS NOTES

Use this space to reflect, celebrate, record answered prayers, and inspire action.

_____
_____
_____
_____
_____
_____
_____
_____

"Gratitude is the song of the soul that remembers who held it through the storm." - Etta Juah

Weekly Check-ins

November
Week 4

WHAT YOU GIVE BACK TO GOD, HE MULTIPLIES
SCRIPTURE OF THE WEEK

"Every good and perfect gift is from above, coming down from the Father of the heavenly lights, who does not change like shifting shadows." — James 1:17

Weekly Reflections

What am I still holding onto that I need to surrender?

Have I given God my willingness today?

What gift have I seen God multiply in my life?

Write down your answers below:

_____
_____
_____
_____
_____
_____
_____
_____

How can I reframe my giving as an act of worship?

_____

What is one area where I need to sow faithfully again?

_____

GRATITUDE PAGE

What are you thankful for this week

_____
_____
_____
_____

ADDITIONAL SEEDS NOTES

Use this space to reflect, celebrate, record answered prayers, and inspire action.

_____
_____
_____
_____
_____
_____
_____

"Gratitude is the song of the soul that remembers who held it through the storm." - Etta Juah

December

JOY & FULFILLMENT
Saying Yes to God's Greatest Gift

And Mary said: 'My soul glorifies the Lord and my spirit rejoices in God my Savior.'" Luke 1:46-47

Woman of the Month: Mary

A Vessel of Joyful Surrender

Mary was young, unnoticed, and likely overlooked by many in her community. But heaven noticed. When the angel Gabriel appeared and called her "highly favored," Mary's whole life changed in an instant. Though afraid and uncertain, she listened. Though confused, she surrendered. Mary didn't have all the answers, but she had a heart ready to obey. Her faith opened the door for the arrival of Christ. In her womb, she carried both a child and the fulfillment of God's promises. Her story teaches us that joy is born not just in comfort, but in calling. And that true fulfillment is found in saying yes to God, even when the journey is unknown. Let Mary's story reminds you: Your obedience to God can carry miracles into the world.

Looking At This Month Devotional

A Willing Heart for a Wondrous Call

"Blessed is she who has believed that the Lord would fulfill His promises to her!"- Luke 1:45. Mary's life changed the moment she said yes to God's plan. Her obedience didn't remove the difficulty, but it birthed joy, hope, and the fulfillment of God's promise to humanity. Joy doesn't mean everything is easy. It often comes wrapped in surrender, sacrifice, and sacred silence. Fulfillment isn't about reaching perfection it's about walking in step with God. As the year closes, reflect: What has God asked of you this year? What have you carried faithfully, even when no one saw? You are still favored. Your yes still matters. God can do something divine through your life. Joy and fulfillment are found in trusting God's plan, even when you don't fully understand it. Say yes, and watch God write miracles through your life.

Further Study

Read more about Mary's story and encounter with God in Luke Chapter 1 - 2.

Prayer

Lord, like Mary, I say yes. Even when I don't understand the full picture, I trust that You are birthing something beautiful through my obedience. Fill my heart with unshakable joy, and let me rejoice in every step of the journey. May my life reflect Your light and my heart overflow with thanksgiving. In Jesus' name, Amen.

Seed of Thought: What if your quiet yes is the answer to someone's desperate prayer?

QUOTE OF THE MONTH

"God's promise over your life will not return void. Believe and carry it."- Etta Juah

Weekly Check-ins

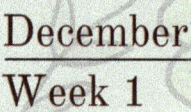

December
Week 1

— • **JOY IS YOUR PORTION LET IT RISE** • —

SCRIPTURE OF THE WEEK

"I am the Lord's servant," Mary answered. "May your word to me be fulfilled."-Luke 1:38

Weekly Reflections

How am I beginning this month emotionally, spiritually, and mentally?

What's one reason I can rejoice today, no matter how I feel?

How can I choose joy in this present moment?

Write down your answers below:

_____
_____
_____
_____
_____
_____
_____
_____

When was the last time I felt joy just by being with God?

_____

Who in my life needs to see the joy of the Lord in me?

_____

GRATITUDE PAGE
What are you thankful for this week

ADDITIONAL SEEDS NOTES
Use this space to reflect, celebrate, record answered prayers, and inspire action.

"God's promise over your life will not return void. Believe and carry it." - Etta Juah

Weekly Check-ins

December
Week 2

FULFILLMENT FOLLOWS FAITH-FILLED SURRENDER
SCRIPTURE OF THE WEEK

"Blessed is she who has believed that the Lord would fulfill His promises to her!" Luke 1:45

Weekly Reflections

What brings me joy in this season of my life?

What am I saying "yes" to this week?

What promise am I seeing unfold or still believing in?

Write down your answers below:

_____
_____
_____
_____
_____
_____
_____

List one tangible occurrence last week.

_____

Write a short prayer of joy, praise, or celebration.

_____

GRATITUDE PAGE
What are you thankful for this week

ADDITIONAL SEEDS NOTES
Use this space to reflect, celebrate, record answered prayers, and inspire action.

"God's promise over your life will not return void. Believe and carry it." - Etta Juah

Weekly Check-ins

December
Week 3

— GOD BIRTHS MIRACLES THROUGH OBEDIENT HEARTS —
SCRIPTURE OF THE WEEK

"For to us a child is born, to us a son is given, and the government will be on His shoulders, And He will be called Wonderful Counselor, Mighty God, Everlasting Father, Prince of Peace.". -Isaiah 9:6

Weekly Reflections

Where is God inviting me to respond with obedience, even when I don't see the full picture?

What miracle might God be preparing to birth through my "yes" to Him today?

How can I align my heart with God's will, like Mary or Isaiah, in trust and surrender?

Write down your answers below:

_____

_____

_____

_____

_____

_____

_____

_____

What small act of obedience am I being nudged toward that could have a lasting impact?

_____

How does knowing Jesus carries the government on His shoulders give me peace in uncertain seasons?

_____

GRATITUDE PAGE

What are you thankful for this week

_____
_____
_____
_____
_____
_____

ADDITIONAL SEEDS NOTES

Use this space to reflect, celebrate, record answered prayers, and inspire action.

_____
_____
_____
_____
_____
_____
_____
_____
_____

"God's promise over your life will not return void. Believe and carry it." - Etta Juah

Weekly Check-ins

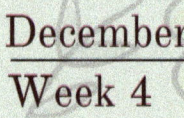

December
Week 4

• YOU WERE CHOSEN TO CARRY SOMETHING DIVINE. •
SCRIPTURE OF THE WEEK

"I have told you this so that my joy may be in you and that your joy may be complete." -John 15:11

Weekly Reflections

What divine assignment or gift do I sense God has entrusted to me?

How can I steward what God has placed in me with faith and humility?

How can I nurture the divine seed within me daily through prayer, obedience, or service?

Write down your answers below:

_____
_____
_____
_____
_____
_____
_____
_____

Write a short prayer of joy, praise, or celebration.

_____

List the tangible gifts that God has used me to give this year.

_____

GRATITUDE PAGE
What are you thankful for this week

ADDITIONAL SEEDS NOTES
Use this space to reflect, celebrate, record answered prayers, and inspire action.

"God's promise over your life will not return void. Believe and carry it." - Etta Juah

FROM YOUR HEAVENLY FATHER

My Beloved Daughter _____

I see you. I know you. I formed you in your mother's womb with care and intention every part of you was made with love (Jeremiah 1:5).

Nothing about you is hidden from Me. Every tear you've cried, I've counted (Psalm 56:8).
You are not forgotten. You are deeply, endlessly loved.
When you feel alone, remember this: I am with you always in the silent nights and the heavy days (Matthew 28:20).
I go before you and I stand behind you (Psalm 139:5).
Nothing, absolutely nothing, can separate you from My love (Romans 8:38-39).
You may feel weary, but I am your strength (Isaiah 41:10).
You may feel broken, but I am close to the brokenhearted (Psalm 34:18).
Call on Me I will answer you (Jeremiah 33:3).
I will never leave you nor forsake you (Deuteronomy 31:6).
My plans for you are good not just good, but full of hope and a future (Jeremiah 29:11). Even when the path feels unclear, trust Me.
I am working all things together for your good (Romans 8:28). Don't fear what lies ahead I already hold your tomorrow.

You are fearfully and wonderfully made (Psalm 139:14). Chosen, Cherished, Mine. You are My masterpiece. So walk boldly in that truth, Let your heart rest in My peace. You were created on purpose, with purpose, for a purpose.

Let Me carry the weight.
Let Me heal the wounds.
Let Me lead your heart.
I delight in you. I rejoice over you with singing (Zephaniah 3:17).
You are Mine now and forever.

With eternal love,
Your Heavenly Father

A LETTER TO MYSELF

Dear Me

About the Author

Etta Juah is a Spirit-led evangelist, writer, and mother with a heart to see women healed, whole, and walking boldly in their God-given identity. Born in West Africa, she brings the depth of her heritage and the beauty of her faith into every page she writes.

After completing her book Seeds of Hope, Etta felt the Holy Spirit stir her to create this companion journal. A sacred space for women to reflect, release, and rediscover God's voice in their everyday lives. With each prompt and prayer, she hopes to encourage women like herself to write their way toward healing and purpose.

Etta Juah

From The Author's Heart

Seeds of Hope for Her is more than a journal it's a sacred journey.

This 12-month faith-filled companion is crafted to help women heal, reflect, and grow in their walk with God. Inside, you'll find powerful scriptures, heartfelt devotionals, inspiring quotes, and daily guided prompts to nurture your soul and strengthen your spirit.

Whether you're seeking clarity, desiring spiritual growth, or longing for a deeper connection with God, this journal was created for you.

Plant the seeds. Water your faith. Trust the process. Watch God move. Every purchase plants a seed of hope.

All proceeds go directly to **A Mother's Touch Foundation**, empowering youth and women through education, mentorship, and healing.

Join us in spreading hope, one seed at a time.

Stay Connected
For more inspiration, updates, and ways to support our mission, reach out through the following channels:
Website: www.ettajuah.com
Email: info@ettajuah.com
A Mother's Touch Foundation: www.amtfcharity.org

We'd love to hear from you!
Thanks for giving yourself to this journey of growth

NOTES

NOTES

NOTES

www.ingramcontent.com/pod-product-compliance
Lightning Source LLC
Chambersburg PA
CBHW061353010526
44107CB00011B/926